SPANISH II UNIT TEN

MW00378593

CONTENTS

Author: **Katherine Engle, M.A.**

Managing Editor: Alan Christopherson, M.S.

Revision Editor: Christine E. Wilson, B.A., M.A.

Illustrators: Steve Ring, Jeri Reed,
Kyle Bennett, Keith Piccolo,
Annette Walker

Graphic Designer: Dawn Tessier

804 N. 2nd Ave. E., Rock Rapids, IA 51246-1759
© MMI by Alpha Omega Publications, Inc. All rights reserved.
LIFEPAC is a registered trademark of Alpha Omega Publications, Inc.

SPANISH II: UNIT TEN
INTRODUCTION

After a review of Unit Nine, Unit Ten's vocabulary lesson opens with the question *¿Qué le pasó?* ("What happened to you?") Upon completing this lesson, you will be able to enter any clinic or emergency room and explain minor symptoms, such as pain or fever. You will also be able to understand a doctor's basic questions concerning your health. With this very practical vocabulary, you could even help someone in need someday.

You will appropriately culminate your study of grammar with two important lessons: relative pronouns and the subjunctive mood. By correctly using relative pronouns, you will be able to create complex sentences that sound natural and mature. Your speech and written communication will sound more "adult."

The subjunctive mood is a difficult one for English speakers to master, because the use of it is quite limited in English. It is, however, an important part of Spanish expression, and it can be mastered through practice and determination. This chapter provides an introduction and an explanation of the forms and usage of the subjunctive mood. You will be able to recognize what kinds of expressions require this mood, translate them, and create subjunctive expressions in Spanish. The use of the subjunctive mood is an indispensable step toward achieving fluent expression.

Section Six describes a research project for you to complete. This project will allow you to conduct your own investigation of another country. The project is designed to encourage you to utilize different types of resources, such as almanacs and atlases. Furthermore, you will research information that perhaps you had not considered before, such as infant mortality and the variety of languages spoken within these Spanish-speaking countries. This project will be informative and interesting as you learn about your chosen country.

OBJECTIVES

Read these objectives. When you have finished this Unit, you should be able to:

1. Be more proficient in using the grammar of Unit Nine.

2. Talk about illness and injury. You will be able to describe basic symptoms and diagnoses of conditions such as the flu and broken limbs.

3. Understand and use the following relative pronouns: *que, quien, cuyo,* and *lo que.*

4. Write complex sentences by correctly using these relative pronouns.

5. Conjugate verbs in the present subjunctive tense.

6. Understand the difference between the subjunctive and indicative moods.

7. Understand the basic use of the subjunctive mood in sentences.

8. Talk in-depth about one Spanish-speaking country of your choice.

I. REVIEW OF UNIT NINE

Review the formation of the imperative. Write the affirmative familiar *(tú)* and formal *(Ud.)* commands of each infinitive.

1.1

	Tú	Ud.
a. leer		
b. buscar		
c. ir		
d. comenzar		
e. hacer		
f. mirar		
g. escribir		
h. ser		
i. pagar		
j. dar		

Make the affirmative commands into negative ones. Be especially mindful of the spelling change of the familiar commands from affirmative to negative.

1.2

	Tú	Ud.
a. leer		
b. buscar		
c. ir		
d. comenzar		
e. hacer		
f. mirar		
g. escribir		
h. ser		
i. pagar		
j. dar		

Write an affirmative and a negative command for each activity pictured. Be mindful of the position of the reflexive pronouns. Use a familiar (*tú*) command for each.

1.3

a. _____

_____

b. _____

_____

c. _____

_____

d. _____

_____

e. _____

_____

f. _____

_____

g. _____

_____

h. _____

_____

Write a logical command for each of the situations described. Use cues within the given statements to determine whether an affirmative or negative command is necessary. Use object pronouns where possible.

1.4 a. Tú estás muy cansada.

_____

b. Ud. no tiene ningún dinero.

_____

c. La bicicleta que acabas de comprar está rota.

_____

d. Es hora de prepararse para ir a clase.

_____

e. Tu sala está sucia.

_____

f. Tienes dolor de cabeza.

_____

g. Ud. está aburrida.

_____

h. Tienes fiebre.

_____

i. Quiere ir al cine con Amalia (Emilio).

_____

j. Estás listo para cenar.

_____

Adult check _____

Initial   Date

Review the adverbial expressions of time. Next to each phrase, write a synonym for that phrase chosen from the list of expressions that you learned in Unit Nine. Do not repeat any of the expressions.

1.5 a. en el presente   _____

b. todavía   _____

c. el día que pasó antes de ayer   _____

d. no a tiempo   _____

e. inmediatamente   _____

f. el último   _____

g. la noche pasada _____

h. pasado _____

i. número uno _____

j. por la noche que viene _____

This time, write an antonym of each phrase.

1.6 a. primero _____

b. tarde _____

c. antes _____

d. todavía _____

e. hoy _____

f. anoche _____

g. no más _____

h. temprano _____

i. ahora mismo _____

j. medianoche _____

Choose and circle the letter of the expression that most logically completes the sentences.

1.7 1. Es importante lavarse las manos ___ comer.
   a. antes   b. antes de   c. antes de que

2. No puedo hacerlo ahora mismo. Lo voy a hacer _____ .
   a. pronto   b. más tarde   c. a esa hora

3. _____ es lunes. Anteayer fue sábado.
   a. Hoy   b. Ayer   c. Mañana

4. Tengo planes. _____ voy al cine.
   a. Ayer   b. Ya   c. Esta noche

5. No dormí bien ____. Hubo una gran tormenta.
   a. esta noche   b. después   c. anoche

6. Esto no pasará otra vez. Ésta es la _____ vez.
   a. última   b. primera   c. próxima

7. Lo necesito ahora mismo. Hazlo _____ .
   a. aún   b. temprano   c. pronto

8. Primero, prepara la cena. _____ pon la mesa.
   a. Todavía   b. Entonces   c. A esa hora

9. ¡_____ son las seis! ¡Cómo vuelan las horas!
   a. Ya   b. Ya no   c. Hoy día

10. No necesité los documentos ayer, ni los necesitaré mañana. Los necesito _____ .
    a. tarde   b. anoche   c. hoy

> **Complete the translations with a logical expression of time.**

1.8 a. He finished it as soon as possible.

     Lo terminó _____ .

     b. Then I told him the answer for the last time.

     _____ le dije la respuesta por _____ .

     c. After seeing the news, I felt sad.

     _____ ver las noticias, me sentí triste.

     d. Bring it to me no later than tonight.

     Tráigamelo no _____ que _____ .

     e. She needs it sooner than that!

     ¡Lo necesita _____ que eso!

     f. They won't be able to see you at that time.

     No podrán verte _____ .

     g. Last week you saw that film.

     _____ viste esa película.

     h. My mom gives me money as soon as I do my chores.

     Mi madre me da el dinero _____ hago los quehaceres.

     i. After he stopped the car, she got out.

     _____ él paró el coche, ella bajó.

     j. She'll speak to him afterward.

     Hablará con él _____ .

✔ Adult check _____

II. ACCIDENTS AND ILLNESSES

¿Qué le pasó?

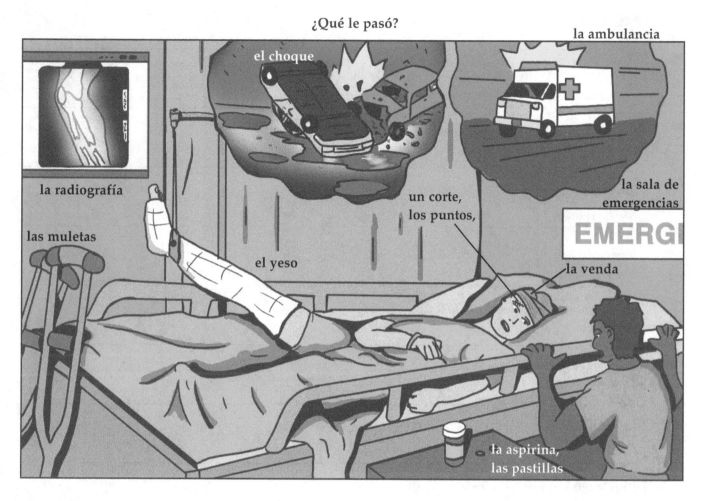

¿Qué ocurrió?

Tuve **un accidente de coche.** Fue terrible. **Me fracturé** la pierna. Recibí **un corte muy profundo** en la frente.

¿Qué hizo entonces?

Fui por **ambulancia** al **hospital.** Llegué a **la sala de emergencias** donde me **hicieron una radiografía** y **me dieron puntos** en la frente. **Las heridas** me duelen mucho, pero no son graves.

¿Quién lo examinó?

El médico me examinó. Me puso **una venda** sobre los cortes de la cabeza. Me informó que la pierna estará en **un yeso** durante seis semanas por lo menos. Me dio **muletas** para que pueda caminar con ellas.

¿Qué le recomendó?

Recomienda que **descanse** y **guarde cama** por una semana. Ahora mismo **me duelen** mucho **las heridas.** Tomo **aspirina** para **el dolor.**

¡Pobrecito! ¡Que se mejore pronto!

Answer the questions in English about the picture and conversation on the preceding page.

2.1   a.   How was this person hurt?

_____

b.   What two different kinds of injuries did he receive?

_____

c.   Where did he seek treatment?

_____

d.   How did he arrive at the hospital?

_____

e.   Who saw him in the hospital?

_____

f.   How was he treated in the hospital?

_____

g.   What did they send home with him?

_____

h.   What does he have to do in order to recover?

_____

i.   What is the aspirin for?

_____

Adult check _____

                                     Initial   Date

¿De qué sufre?

Me caí en la escalera. **Me torcí** el tobillo. Me duele mucho.

¿Qué hizo entonces?

Visité **el consultorio de la médica.** El tobillo está **hinchado** y tiene **una contusión**. Ella me puso **una venda** y dice que voy a **recuperarme** pronto.

¿Qué le recomendó?

Tengo que llevar la venda durante unos días. Debo tener cuidado cuando camino.

¡Qué lástima! ¡Que se recupere pronto!

Answer the comprehension questions in English.

2.2   a.   How was she hurt?

_____

b.   What was the extent of her injuries?

_____

c.   Did she have to go to the hospital? If not, where did she go?

_____

d.   How is her injury being treated?

_____

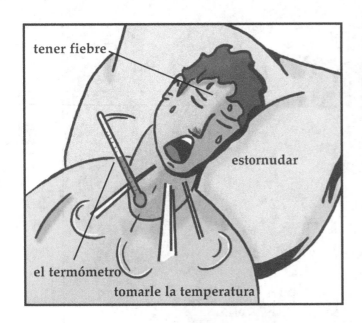

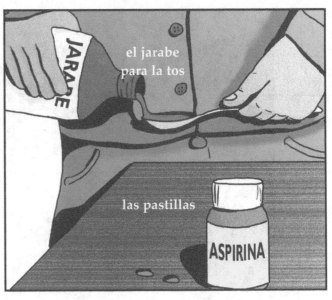

¿De qué sufre?

Estoy seguro de que tengo **la pulmonía** o **la bronquitis.** Me duele la cabeza. **Tengo fiebre** de ciento un grados. **Estornudo** y **toso** constantemente. Tengo **náuseas**; quiero **vomitar** todo el tiempo.

¿Fue a la clínica?

Fui **a la clínica. Una enfermera** me examinó. Ella **me tomó la temperatura** con **un termómetro**, y **me tomó el pulso**. Entonces el médico **consultó** conmigo. Le describí todos mis **síntomas**. El médico me **auscultó** con el **estetoscopio.**

¿Qué le recomendó?

Me dio **una receta** para **antibióticos.** Dijo que tengo **la gripe.** También me **recetó jarabe para la tos.** Tengo que **quedarme en cama** hasta que **me mejore.**

¡Pobrecito! ¡Que se sienta mejor pronto!

Complete the comprehension questions in English.

2.3   a.   Why does he think he has pneumonia or bronchitis?

            _____

        b.   Where did he go for help?

            _____

        c.   Who saw him there?

            _____

        d.   What procedures did they follow to diagnose him?

            _____

        e.   Name two typical symptoms of the flu that he mentioned.

            _____

        f.   What two medications were prescribed for him?

            _____

        g.   What does he have to do when he gets home?

            _____

✔ Adult check _____

                                       Initial   Date

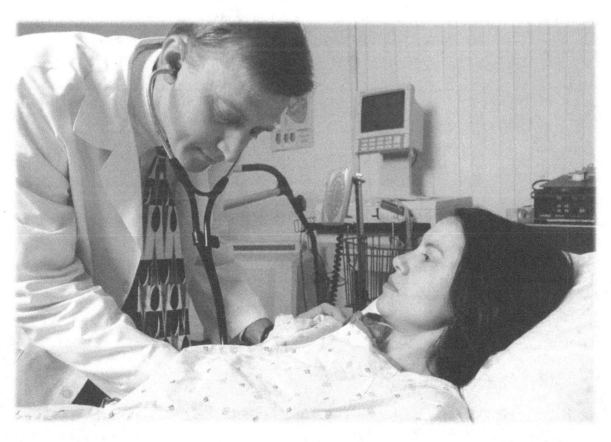

Complete the following vocabulary list below. First, fill in the easiest cognates. Next, use the stories and the illustrations throughout this Unit to fill in those words whose meanings you can derive from the context. Only then, use a dictionary to complete the list.

2.4

1. la herida _____
2. torcerse _____
3. el tobillo _____
4. la muñeca _____
5. la contusión _____
6. caerse _____
7. el corte _____
8. profundo _____
9. la enfermedad _____
10. la pulmonía _____
11. la bronquitis _____
12. el resfriado _____
13. la gripe _____
14. el síntoma _____
15. hinchado _____
16. me duele _____
17. la fiebre _____
18. estornudar _____
19. toser _____
20. vomitar _____
21. las náuseas _____
22. el diagnóstico _____
23. el reconocimiento _____
24. examinar _____
25. el (la) médico(a) _____

26. el (la) enfermero(a) _____
27. el hospital _____
28. la clínica _____
29. tomarle la temperatura _____
30. el termómetro _____
31. tomarle el pulso _____
32. el estetoscopio _____
33. hacerse una radiografía _____
34. la ambulancia _____
35. darle puntos a _____
36. el consultorio _____
37. la cura _____
38. las muletas _____
39. la venda _____
40. la curita _____
41. el yeso _____
42. enyesar _____
43. vendar _____
44. descansar _____
45. guardar cama _____
46. la aspirina _____
47. el antibiótico _____
48. la pastilla _____
49. recuperarse _____
50. recetar _____

51. la receta _____

52. el pañuelo de papel _____

53. el jarabe para la tos _____

54. los deseos_____

55. ¡Que se (te) mejore(s) pronto! _____

56. ¡Que se (te) recupere(s) pronto! _____

57. ¡Pobrecito! _____

58. ¡Qué lástima! _____

59. ¡Que se (te) sienta(s) mejor pronto! _____

✔ Adult check _____
　　　　　　　　　　　　　Initial　　　　　　　　　　　Date

OPTIONAL ACTIVITY A: Carefully study the vocabulary list at the end of the Unit. Using the list as a reference, make a set of 3 x 5" flashcards. Label each card with the Spanish word on the front and the English translation on the back.

✔ Adult check _____
　　　　　　　　　　　　　Initial　　　　　　　　　　　Date

Complete the translations with an appropriate vocabulary term.

2.5 a.　The nurse determines that you have a fever by taking your temperature.

_____ determina que tiene _____ tomándole

_____ .

b.　Put a band-aid on that cut!

¡Ponte _____ en ese _____ !

c.　The doctor had to put 28 stitches on that deep cut.

_____ tuvo que _____ en ese

_____ .

d.　The doctor will examine you (friendly) in his office.

_____ va a _____ en su _____ .

e.　He's got a bruise on his ankle.

Tiene _____ en _____ .

f.　Sneeze into the tissue, please.

Favor de _____ dentro del _____ .

13

g. He has all the symptoms of pneumonia.

Tiene todos _____ de _____ .

h. I don't have a doctor, so I'll go to the clinic.

No tengo _____ , por eso voy a _____ .

i. The X-ray shows that you broke your arm.

_____ muestra que _____ .

j. He only twisted his ankle. Why does he need crutches?

Solamente _____ ¿Por qué necesita _____ ?

THE EXPRESSION "ME DUELE"

Me duele ("it hurts me") works grammatically just like *Me gusta(n)* ("I like").

Answer the questions.

2.6 a. If you like *one* thing, which form of *gustar* do you use? _____

b. If you like *more than one* thing, which form of *gustar* do you use? _____

Me duele really translates as "It hurts me." So the sentence *Me duele la cabeza* translates word-for-word as "My head hurts me."

c. What is the true subject of this Spanish sentence? _____

d. Translate this sentence: *Me duelen las piernas.*

_____

e. What is the true subject of this sentence? _____

f. Why did we use the *ellos* form of the verb this time? _____

_____

Basically, if one body part hurts (or doesn't hurt), use *(no) me duele.*

If more than one (feet, for example) hurts (or doesn't hurt), use *(no) me duelen.*

Use the same indirect object pronouns *(me, te, le, nos, les)* as you would with *gustar.*

Translate into Spanish. Use a form of *duele* or *duelen* with the appropriate indirect object pronoun in each sentence.

2.7   1.   My head hurts.   a. _____

           My head doesn't hurt.   b. _____

           His head hurts.   c. _____

       2.   My feet hurt.   a. _____

           Do your (friendly) feet hurt?   b. _____

           Her feet hurt.   c. _____

       3.   What hurts you? (friendly)   a. _____

           What hurts us?   b. _____

           What hurts them?   c. _____

       4.   My throat doesn't hurt.   a. _____

           My throat hurts.   b. _____

           María's throat hurts.   c. _____

       5.   My fingers hurt.   a. _____

           Do your (formal) fingers hurt?   b. _____

           My fingers don't hurt.   c. _____

Complete the crossword puzzle.

2.8

ACROSS
3. the illnesses
7. the crash
9. the aspirin
14. a bruise
16. the crutches
20. the desires
21. Poor thing!
22. the injuries, wounds
25. the wrist
26. the ambulance

DOWN
1. the cast
2. it hurts me
3. the pneumonia
4. the cut
5. to recuperate
6. the band-aid
8. the bandage
10. the symptoms
11. to fall down
12. to stay in bed

13. a prescription
15. the fever
17. to cough
18. to prescribe
19. doctor
23. to suffer
24. What a shame!
25. the cure

¿Es un síntoma, una enfermedad, una herida o una cura? Label each term as a symptom, an illness, an injury, or a medical treatment in Spanish.

2.9 a. _____ la gripe

b. _____ romperse

c. _____ un corte

d. _____ una venda

e. _____ la contusión

f. _____ el resfriado

g. _____ darle puntos a

h. _____ el antibiótico

i. _____ estornudar

j. _____ toser

Determine what each person needs, based on the situation you read. Describe your decision in complete Spanish sentences.

2.10 a. Me duele la cabeza. ¿Qué necesito?

_____

b. Hay un corte pequeño en el dedo de Mariana. ¿Qué debe llevar?

_____

c. Me duele mucho toser. ¿Qué tomo?

_____

d. Se torció el tobillo. ¿Qué debe hacer ella?

_____

e. Creo que me fracturé el brazo. ¿A quién necesito visitar?

_____

f. El corte es muy grande y profundo. ¿Adónde tiene que ir tu hermano?

_____

g. Estornudas. ¿Qué usas?

_____

h. El médico dice que la pulmonía de Timoteo es muy grave. ¿Dónde se quedará?

_____

i. Alicia no puede caminar con ese yeso. ¿Qué necesita?

_____

j. ¿Cómo puede determinar la médica que tienes fiebre?

_____

Choose and circle the most logical response to each question.

2.11
1. ¿De qué sufres?

    a. la receta   b. la bronquitis   c. recuperarse

2. ¿Qué le recomienda la enfermera?

    a. caerse   b. torcerse   c. descansar

3. ¿Adónde vas?

    a. la pulmonía   b. la contusión   c. al consultorio

4. ¿Qué le recomienda el médico?

    a. guardar cama   b. la gripe   c. doler

5. ¿Qué te pasó?

    a. me caí   b. me auscultó   c. me aconsejó

6. ¿Para qué es la receta?

    a. para tomarle la presión   b. para vendar   c. para mejorarse

7. ¿Cuál es la temperatura?

    a. ciento un grados   b el resfriado   c. veinte pañuelos de papel

8. ¿Cuántos puntos te dio?

    a. ciento un grados   b. treinta y dos   c. por lo menos dos días

9. ¿Para qué son los antibióticos?

    a. una herida   b. una enfermedad   c. un choque

10. ¿Qué causó la contusión?

    a. un resfriado   b. hinchado   c. un choque

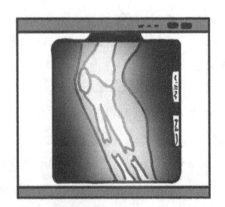

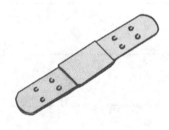
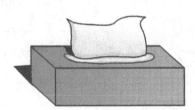

Label each illustration in Spanish with a vocabulary term that identifies the item, the action, or what function the item performs. Do not repeat any terms.

2.12

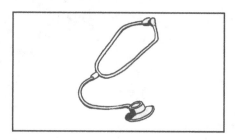

a. _____

b. _____

c. _____

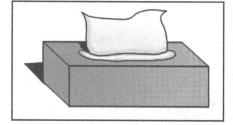

d. _____

e. _____

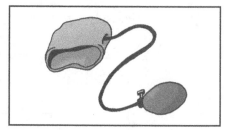

f. _____

g. _____

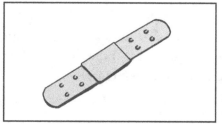

h. _____

i. _____

j. _____

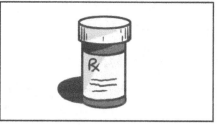

k. _____

l. _____

m. _____

n. _____

o. _____

Fill in the blank with the correct word(s) needed to complete each sentence. Choose each term only once. Two will not be used.

2.13

un resfriado	una ambulancia	una venda	una curita
un termómetro	muletas	un estetoscopio	una enfermera
el jarabe	una receta	antibióticos	la fiebre

a. Necesito _____ para auscultar.

b. Necesito _____ para tomarle la temperatura.

c. Necesito _____ para obtener las pastillas.

d. Necesito _____ para caminar porque tengo una pierna rota.

e. Necesito _____ para cubrir el corte.

f. Necesito _____ para la tos.

g. Necesito _____ porque tengo un tobillo hinchado.

h. Necesito _____ porque estoy en el hospital y tengo dolor.

i. Necesito _____ porque tengo la gripe.

j. Necesito _____ porque hay una emergencia.

Describe an experience you had similar to those in this section. Include any injuries or symptoms you suffered. Describe how you got better and who helped you. Write at least ten complete Spanish sentences, using the past tenses: preterit, imperfect, present perfect, pluperfect.

2.14 _____

_____

_____

_____

_____

_____

_____

_____

_____

_____

_____

_____

_____

_____

_____

_____

OPTIONAL ACTIVITY B: Role-play a scene in an emergency room with a learning partner. The "patient" should complain of at least three symptoms specific to a particular injury or illness. The "doctor" and/or "nurse" should explain every procedure he or she performs on the patient. At the end, the "doctor" should make a diagnosis and a recommendation for recovery. Write a dialogue on the lines below, if you wish.

_____

_____

_____

_____

_____

_____

_____

_____

_____

_____

_____

_____

_____

_____

✔ Adult check _____

Initial   Date

Read each situation with your classmates to make sure you understand everything. Then have your instructor randomly select one of the topics for you to respond to verbally.

2.15 a. Eres médico(a). El paciente se queja de un dolor de cabeza y una fiebre. Haz un diagnóstico.

b. Eres el paciente. Crees que sufres de la pulmonía. ¿Qué le dices a la enfermera?

c. Te caíste de un árbol. No puedes caminar porque te duele mucho la pierna. ¿Cómo explicas esto al médico?

d. Estás en el supermercado cuando de repente (suddenly) te sientes náuseas. ¿Qué le dices a tu compañero?

e. Tu amigo está en el hospital. Hace muchas semanas que está muy enfermo. Va a volver a casa en dos días. ¿Qué le desea?

✔ Adult check _____

Initial   Date

Exercise 1. Listen to each statement carefully. Match its letter to one of the illustrations below. [CD–F, Track 1]

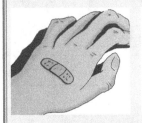 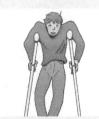  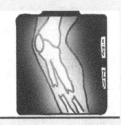 

1. _____ 2. _____ 3. _____ 4. _____ 5. _____

  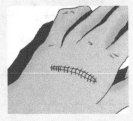 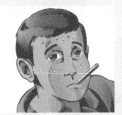 

6. _____ 7. _____ 8. _____ 9. _____ 10. _____

Exercise 2. Choose and circle the most logical response to the statements you hear. [CD–F, Track 2]

1. a. Te la fracturaste.
   b. Sufres de un resfriado.
   c. Necesitas una venda.

2. a. Vaya en la ambulancia.
   b. Visita al dentista.
   c. Sufres de la gripe.

3. a. Posiblemente necesitas un pañuelo de papel.
   b. Toma los antibióticos.
   c. No te preocupes. Te lo torciste.

4. a. Ponte una venda.
   b. Guarda cama.
   c. ¿Le dieron puntos?

5. a. ¿Te cortaste?
   b. ¿Te rompiste?
   c. ¿Te enyesaron?

6. a. ¿Te caíste?
   b. Necesitas una ambulancia.
   c. Tienes bronquitis.

7. a. Voy a examinarte.
   b. Sigue esta receta.
   c. No está el médico.

8. a. Aquí están las muletas.
   b. Le pongo una venda.
   c. Voy a toser.

9. a. Por favor, siéntese.
   b. Acaba de vomitar.
   c. Vaya a la clínica.

10. a. Necesitas una curita.
    b. El tobillo está hinchado.
    c. Necesitas antibióticos.

Exercise 3. Suggest a different remedy for each sufferer. [CD–F, Track 3]

a. _____

b. _____

c. _____

d. _____

e. _____

f. _____

g. _____

h. _____

i. _____

j. _____

✔ Adult check _____

                               Initial   Date

Review the material in this section in preparation for the Self Test. The Self Test will check your mastery of this particular section. The items missed on this Self Test will indicate specific areas where restudy is needed for mastery.

SELF TEST 2

2.01   Match the Spanish to the English. (1 pt. each)

1. _____ el consultorio del médico   a. to recuperate

2. _____ profundo   b. swollen

3. _____ hinchado   c. it hurts me

4. _____ recetar   d. the thermometer

5. _____ ¡Qué lástima!   e. the doctor's office

6. _____ recuperarse   f. the cold

7. _____ el termómetro   g. deep

8. _____ el resfriado   h. What a shame!

9. _____ me duele   i. the band-aid

10. _____ la curita   j. to prescribe

2.02   Now match the English to the Spanish. (1 pt. each)

1. _____ the cough syrup   a. las muletas

2. _____ to examine   b. el jarabe para la tos

3. _____ the cut   c. ¡Que se sienta mejor pronto!

4. _____ to cough   d. la cura

5. _____ to give stitches   e. examinar

6. _____ Hope you feel better soon!   f. la enfermedad

7. _____ the fever   g. toser

8. _____ the cure   h. darle puntos a

9. _____ the illness   i. la fiebre

10. _____ the crutches   j. el corte

2.03   Write the English equivalent of each vocabulary term. (1 pt. each)

a. las náuseas _____

b. la ambulancia _____

c. ¡Que se recupere pronto! _____

d. los deseos _____

e. el reconocimiento _____

f. la gripe _____

g. las heridas _____

h. la receta _____

i. descansar _____

j. la muñeca _____

2.04   **Write the Spanish equivalent of each vocabulary term.** (1 pt. each)

   a.   the broken leg _____

   b.   Poor thing!   _____

   c.   the bruise _____

   d.   to stay in bed _____

   e.   to sneeze _____

   f.   the cold (illness) _____

   g.   the symptoms _____

   h.   the diagnosis _____

   i.   the headache _____

   j.   the bone _____

2.05   **Study the picture above. Write the Spanish term on the line for each item numbered on the picture.**
       (1 pt. each)

   1. _____   6. _____

   2. _____   7. _____

   3. _____   8. _____

   4. _____   9. _____

   5. _____   10. _____

2.06   **Complete the sentences with a Spanish term from this Unit's vocabulary.** (1 pt. each)

    a.   Para el dolor de cabeza, debe tomar _____ .

    b.   La niña tiene _____ de ciento dos grados.

    c.   Las náuseas terminaron cuando _____ .

    d.   Después del accidente, pasa tres semanas en _____ .

    e.   _____ para la pulmonía es tomar antibióticos.

    f.   A veces es necesario viajar a la sala de emergencias por _____ .

    g.   Toma _____ para una tos fuerte.

    h.   El médico hace _____ de bronquitis.

    i.   El reconocimiento tiene lugar en _____ .

    j.   ¿Estás enfermo? ¡Que se _____ !

2.07   **Translate the following sentences into Spanish.** (2 pts. each)

    a.   I stay in bed when I have a cold. _____

        _____

    b.   The nurse doesn't prescribe antibiotics. _____

        _____

    c.   The doctor examines serious wounds in the emergency room._____

        _____

    d.   I have nausea. I'm going to throw up! _____

        _____

    e.   Manolito wears a band-aid on his cut._____

        _____

    f.   The nurse stitches the deep cut. _____

        _____

    g.   She fell down and received a bruise on her leg._____

        _____

    h.   Wear a bandage on your ankle._____

        _____

    i.   Some symptoms of the flu are a cough, nausea, and a fever. _____

        _____

    j.   Poor thing! You have bronchitis. _____

        _____

64	
	80

Score   _____

Adult check   _____
                         Initial   Date

III. RELATIVE PRONOUNS

The English and Spanish languages both use relative pronouns. The job of a relative pronoun is to connect two clauses, phrases, or sentences which have something in common. They connect and relate the second clause to the first.

Some common English relative pronouns are *that, which,* and *who*. For example, here are two related sentences.

> **I bought a book.**
> **The book is good.**

Here are the same two sentences, connected by a relative pronoun into one sentence.

> **I bought a book *that* is good.**

Relative pronouns give our speech and writing a more flowing nature. They allow us to create complex sentences and introduce more variety to our sentence structure. Read the following:

> **I see Carla has a dog.**
> **The dog is brown.**

There is certainly nothing grammatically wrong with these sentences. Compare how they sound, however, once they are linked into one sentence by a relative pronoun.

> **I see Carla has a dog *that* is brown.**

Everyday conversation is more likely to sound this way. Once you are proficient at using relative pronouns, however, your previous expression (your compositions, etc.) may seem almost stilted in tone. You won't feel that you are communicating well without relative pronouns.

Combine each pair of English sentences into one sentence with a relative pronoun. Read each pair of sentences, then think about how you would join each pair, using words like *that, who,* and *which*. Consider how the sentences sound as you link them. Write the one new sentence, in English, in the space provided.

3.1 a. My sister took the cookie.
The cookie was on the table.

_____

b. We saw the movie.
The movie played Saturday night.

_____

c. I can't see that bald man.
You are talking about that bald man.

_____

d. Alonso is sixteen years old.
Alonso just bought an automobile.

_____

e. My mom bought the gold shoes.
She had to return them the next day.

_____

f. Betty's cousin has pneumonia.
He is in the hospital.

_____

g. Here is a prescription for antibiotics.
The antibiotics will help make you feel better.

_____

h. Oven cleaner is a caustic chemical.
Oven cleaner burns the skin.

_____

i. Consuelo is a friend.
I made a birthday cake (for Consuelo).

_____

j. Mr. Allen spends winters in Cancún.
Mr. Allen is a retired dentist.

_____

There are two kinds of clauses into which relative pronouns fit: **restrictive** and **nonrestrictive**.

Restrictive clauses make reference to a _specific_ noun. They follow the relative pronoun in a sentence and may clarify a single noun from a group.

> **The car that we just bought doesn't run.**

The speaker may own a few cars. The restrictive phrase _that we just bought_ specifies about which car he or she is talking. It could also refger to the only car the speaker owns. It doesn't single out one car among all the other cars he owns, but one among all cars in existence.

Nonrestrictive clauses provide additional information for an already known entity. They also follow the relative pronoun. For example:

> **My dad, who's 75 years old, runs five miles every day.**
> **Mr. Ramirez, who's my favorite professor, teaches biology at the university.**

In each case, the subject was specific and already known to the listener. The nonrestrictive clauses _who's 75 years old_ and _who's my favorite teacher_ embellish the picture the speaker is trying to paint.

> **Identify the restrictive clause in this sentence.**

3.2   a.   I need a job that pays very well. _____

        The speaker specified which kind of job was needed with a restrictive clause. (Restrictive clauses are more common than nonrestrictive clauses in English and Spanish.)

Identify the nonrestrictive clauses in each sentence.

    b.   My friend's truck, which is brand-new, is in the shop again. _____

    c.   Pedro's girlfriend, who is working late at the supermarket, can't make it to the party.

_____

> **Decide whether each of the following sentences contains a restrictive or nonrestrictive clause, or no restrictive clause at all. Name the type of clause in the space provided (or write *none*) and write that clause in the blank as well.**

3.3   a.   The bride wore the same gown that her mother had worn forty years ago._____

_____

    b.   Did you hear the siren that went off at six o'clock? _____

_____

    c.   Ronaldo ate dinner in a restaurant that was very elegant. _____

_____

    d.   The little girl was wearing the dress that her mother had made for her. _____

_____

    e.   Can't you see that? _____

    f.   Unfortunately, Beto, whose parents are college professors, failed the math test. _____

_____

    g.   I heard that dog barking all night. _____

    h.   We follow a strict diet that is low in cholesterol. _____

    i.   The new building that's on the corner was robbed last night. _____

_____

    j.   Whose bike is this? It needs to be moved. _____

Now that we have reviewed what English relative pronouns do and how they are used in sentences, let's discuss some Spanish relative pronouns.

que (that, who, which)

- most commonly used
- refers to people and things
- may be used for things after prepositions like *de, para, con*, etc.

Notice that, unlike the interrogative *¿qué?*, this *que* does not have an accent mark. After a preposition, the relative pronoun *que* refers only to (non-human) things.

Connect these Spanish sentences into one sentence with the relative pronoun *que*. Then translate each new sentence into English.

Examples: Compré el vestido.
Este vestido era el más elegante.
Compré el vestido que era el más elegante.
I bought the dress that was the most elegant.

Recomiendo al doctor Ramírez.
Es mi médico favorito.
Recomiendo al doctor Ramírez, que es mi médico favorito.
I recommend Doctor Ramírez, who is my favorite doctor.

Aquí están las herramientas especiales.
Voy a reparar la computadora con estas herramientas especiales.
Aquí están las herramientas especiales con que voy a reparar la computadora.
Here are the special tools that (which) I am going to repair the computer with.
(Literally: Here are the special tools *with which* I am going to repair the computer.)

3.4   a.   Rompí el vaso.
Te gusta mucho este vaso.

_____

_____

b.   Me mostrará el anillo.
Cuesta ochocientos dólares.

_____

_____

c.   Obtenemos el puesto.
Necesitamos el puesto muchísimo.

_____

_____

d. Perdiste la foto.
   Te di la foto.

   _____

   _____

e. ¿Publicó esas mentiras?
   Ella dijo esas mentiras.

   _____

   _____

f. Conocemos a una secretaria.
   La secretaria habla francés y español.

   _____

   _____

~~~~~~

> **quien(es)** (who, that)
>
> ■ used only with people
> ■ normally used with prepositions
>   such as **a** (*a quien[es]* – to whom)
>   or **con** (*con quien[es]* – with whom)

Examples: The lady that (who) you were speaking with is my mother.
(Literally / Formal English: The lady with whom you were speaking is my mother.)
La mujer con quien hablabas es mi madre.

The man that (who) you should pay the bill to is wearing a red tie.
(Literally / Formal English): The man to whom you should pay the bill is wearing a red
   tie.)
El hombre a quien deberías pagar la cuenta lleva una corbata roja.

The children that (who) you bought the ice cream for are very happy.
(Literally / Formal English): The children for whom you bought the ice cream are very
   happy.
Los niños para quienes compraste el helado están muy contentos.

> Translate the following sentences into Spanish.

3.5 a. Who is that man that you were speaking to?

   _____

b. The friends, who I'm going to the party with, are bringing the soft drinks.

   _____

c. I'm not sure who the children arrived with.

_____

d. I ate lunch with Mr. Balnear, who I used to work with.

_____

e. Marcos is the man that I told you (plu.) about.

_____

f. The lady that I was arguing (discutir) with was my boss.

_____

> **Decide whether the relative pronoun *que* or *quien* completes each sentence.**

3.6   a. La mujer de _____ hablo no está aquí ahora.

b. El suéter _____ Luisa compró es feo.

c. No sabía _____ no te gustaba el helado.

d. Ricardo es el hombre para _____ compré el chocolate.

e. Esperamos un mes, _____ no es mucho tiempo.

f. Devolviste el reloj _____ compraste ayer.

g. Mira las nubes _____ están pasando.

h. Muchos ancianos, _____ vienen a votar, se oponen a la nueva ley.

i. El pobre señor, _____ acaba de enfermar, murió anteayer.

j. Necesito un coche _____ funcione bien.

---

cuyo(a)(s) (whose)

■ This is the non-interrogative (non-question) form of the word *whose*.

■ **Cuyo** is actually a relative adjective, and it must agree in number and gender with what is owned.

> **Analyze the examples.**

3.7   *La casa, cuyos cuartos son muy grandes, cuesta mucho.* The house, whose rooms are very big, costs a lot.

a. What noun does *cuyos* refer to? _____

b. What Spanish noun, however, does *cuyos* agree with? _____

La señora cuyo jardín yo planté está de vacaciones. The lady, whose garden I planted, is on vacation.

c. Why is *cuyo* masculine, if the sentence is about a lady? _____

Translate the following into Spanish. Use a form of *cuyo* in each of your answers.

3.8 a. Carlitos, whose plane is arriving late, is waiting in the cafeteria.

_____

b. My mom, whose office is in our home, is an accountant.

_____

c. I know the woman whose phone number you have.

_____

d. The student, whose assignments are here, needs to pick them up (*recogerlas*).

_____

e. That author, whose books are famous, gave an interview on TV.

_____

As you have learned, "whose" may be expressed in the middle of a sentence with a form of the relative pronoun *cuyo*. "Whose," an interrogative that usually comes at the beginning of a question, is expressed by *¿De quién(es)?* The English word order may need to be changed somewhat in order to use this expression correctly in Spanish. Note the literal translations given in the sample sentences.

Roberto, *cuyo* hijo es mi vecino, recomendó este libro.
Roberto, *whose* son is my neighbor, recommended this book.

¿*De quién* es este libro?
Whose book is it? (Literally: Of whom / Whose is this book?)

¿*De quién* es el libro que lees?
Whose book are you reading? (Literally: Of whom / Whose is the book that you are reading?)

¿*De quiénes* son los niños que vienen a la fiesta?
Whose children are coming to the party? (Literally: Of whom / Whose are the children who are coming to the party?)

Use *de quién(es)* **in these questions.**

3.9   a.   Whose lunch did you take yesterday?

   _____

   b.   Do you know whose magazine this is?

   _____

   c.   Whose car is he driving? _____

   d.   Whose lights are turned on? _____

   e.   Whose radio is that? _____

Lo que (that which, what)

■ The relative pronoun *lo que* is used to refer back to an idea or a concept previously mentioned, rather than a specific noun. It has only the one form.

Note the differences between the relative pronoun *que* (referring to a specific noun) and *lo que* (not referring to a specific noun).

No entiendo el poema *que* **escribió Marta.**
I don't understand the poem *that* Marta wrote.

No entiendo *lo que* **dijo Marta.**
I don't understand *what* Marta said.

In the first example, *que* refers to *el poema*. In the second sentence, *lo que* refers to a concept or an idea.

■ The relative pronoun *lo que* may be combined with *todo* to indicate "all that" or everything that."

Compré *todo lo que* **necesitaba para ir de camping la semana que viene.**
I bought *everything that* I needed in order to go camping next week.

■ *Lo que* can also come at the beginning of a sentence. Do not confuse this with *¿Qué?* or *¿Cuál?*, which are interrogative pronouns that appear in questions.

¿*Qué* quieres saber?
What do you want to know?

***Lo que* quiero saber es la verdad.**
What I want to know is the truth.

Which sentence needs *que*, and which needs *lo que*?

3.10 a. _____ I read what (that which) I need to for class.

_____ There's the book that I'm reading for class.

b. _____ We do the chores that Mother told us to do.

_____ We do what Mother told us to do.

c. _____ Is that the show she was talking about?

_____ Is that what she was talking about?

d. _____ Did they bring the things she asked for?

_____ Did they bring what she asked for?

Translate the following sentences into Spanish. Use the *tú* form for "you" throughout this activity.

3.11 a. I don't know what you want. Tell me what you want.

_____

b. What I want is to find a good job.

_____

c. What did you buy?

_____

d. I bought the cereal that you recommended.

_____

e. Tell me all that you bought.

_____

Summarize what you have reviewed.

3.12 a. What do relative pronouns "do" in a sentence? _____

b. What kinds of clauses do relative pronouns join? _____

Define each of the two clauses.

c. _____

d. _____

Make a short list of the relative pronouns we have studied here. Include the English meaning of each pronoun.

e. _____

f. _____

g. _____

h. _____

i. Which relative pronoun refers only and specifically to humans? _____

Translate the English words into Spanish.

3.13   a. The student *who* came to see me is studying Spanish.

El estudiante _____ vino a verme estudia el español.

b. The church *that* I attend is near my home.

La iglesia a _____ asisto está cerca de mi casa.

c. The ladies *that* I made these copies *for* have already left.

Las mujeres _____ hice estas fotocopias ya han salido.

d. *What* did you want to buy at the handicrafts market?

¿ _____ querías comprar en el mercado de artesanías?

e. I wanted to buy *everything that* I saw there.

Quería comprar _____ vi allí.

f. *Whose* X-ray is this?

¿ _____ es esta radiografía?

g. Miguel, *whom* I was going to go to the game *with*, has to work late tonight.

Miguel, _____ iba a ir al partido, tiene que trabajar tarde esta noche.

h. The dog *that* we saw is my cousin's.

El perro _____ vimos es de mi primo.

i. I have a friend *whose* parents are traveling in Europe right now.

Tengo un amigo _____ padres viajan en Europa ahora mismo.

j. I will do *what* you want.

Haré _____ quieres.

k. *Whose* child is this?

¿ _____ es este niño?

l. *Who* gave you that ring?

¿ _____ te dio ese anillo?

m. I know a nurse *whose* daughter has the same illness as my daughter.

Conozco a una enfermera _____ hija tiene la misma enfermedad que mi hija.

Have you noticed that the sentences you have read and created are much longer than you may have written before? That's a good thing! Relative pronouns *connect* ideas; therefore, you are bound to write longer, complex sentences. Your expression now sounds more mature.

Exercise 1. Listen to each Spanish sentence. Decide if that sentence contains a restrictive or nonrestrictive clause. Circle *Restrictive* or *Nonrestrictive*. [CD–F, Track 4]

a.	Restrictive	Nonrestrictive	f.	Restrictive	Nonrestrictive
b.	Restrictive	Nonrestrictive	g.	Restrictive	Nonrestrictive
c.	Restrictive	Nonrestrictive	h.	Restrictive	Nonrestrictive
d.	Restrictive	Nonrestrictive	i.	Restrictive	Nonrestrictive
e.	Restrictive	Nonrestrictive	j.	Restrictive	Nonrestrictive

Exercise 2. Decide which person(s) or thing(s) the relative pronoun is referring to by listening to each sentence. Circle your choice. [CD–F, Track 5]

1.	a. el jefe	b. el rascacielos	c. la oficina
2.	a. el hambre	b. los pobres	c. el pueblo
3.	a. el amigo	b. el hermano	c. Roberto
4.	a. Rosa y Anita	b. sus primas	c. los jóvenes
5.	a. la sala	b. el cuero	c. los zapatos
6.	a. mis favoritas	b. las galletas	c. el chocolate
7.	a. las verduras	b. mi jardín	c. la sopa
8.	a. la mujer	b. Ramón	c. las flores
9.	a. mi madre	b. la oficina	c. mis hermanitos
10.	a. los trenes	b. el lugar	c. la estación

Review the material in this section in preparation for the Self Test. This Self Test will check your mastery of this particular section as well as your knowledge of the previous sections.

SELF TEST 3

3.01   **Complete each sentence with the correct relative pronoun.** (1 pt. each)

   a.   Pasamos una calle _____ se estaba reparando ahora.

   b.   Repita _____ acaba de decir.

   c.   Conoce a una enfermera _____ quiere ser médica.

   d.   ¿Quién es la señora a _____ hablabas?

   e.   ¿Cómo se llama el libro de _____ hablas?

   f.   Miré _____ pasaba.

   g.   Nadamos en el mar _____ es muy frío en mayo.

   h.   No les gusta la película _____ vieron ayer.

   i.   El supermercado, _____ precios son buenos, ofrece las frutas más frescas de la ciudad.

   j.   ¿Es ése el vaso _____ echaste al suelo?

   k.   En la escuela hacemos _____ nos manda el profesor.

   l.   No puede recordar _____ vio esa tarde.

   m.   El juguete _____ compré ayer no funciona.

   n.   Rosita es la niña para _____ compré este juguete.

3.02   **Combine the sentences in each group, making just one final sentence from all. Use a relative pronoun in each case.** (2 pts. each)

   a.   La biblioteca tiene muchos libros.
         Ofrece los libros a toda la gente.

         _____

   b.   La televisión está en la basura.
         La televisión no funciona.

         _____

   c.   Como.
         Me gusta comer.

         _____

   d.   Mi amigo Juan es muy inteligente.
         Recibe una beca de la universidad.

         _____

   e.   El ladrón se escapó.
         La policía no lo encontró.

         _____

39

f. Los esfuerzos del estudiante son grandes.
    El estudiante tendrá mucho éxito.

    _____

g. Mi padre es profesor de matemáticas.
    Vive cerca de la universidad.

    _____

h. Pasaba mucho tiempo escuchando la música.
    Las melodías de la música me calmaban.

    _____

i. Elena llama a su familia todos los sábados.
    Elena vive lejos de su casa.

    _____

j. ¿De quién es el coche?
    El coche está estacionado en mi césped.

    _____

k. Trajo al perro.
    Encontró al perro en la calle.

    _____

l. Escribimos lo importante.
    Lo consideramos importante.

    _____

m. Su tío siempre tiene una cita los viernes.
    Su tío es muy divertido.

    _____

32 / 40

Score _____

Adult check _____
               Initial   Date

SPANISH II: LIFEPAC TEST UNIT TEN

Name _____

Date _____

Score _____

$\dfrac{96}{120}$

1.   **Choose and circle the correct relative pronoun.** (1 pt. each)

   a. Vendí el coche (que / quien) compré el año pasado.

   b. La mujer, con (que / quien) hablo, es muy simpática.

   c. ¿Puedes mostrarme los carteles (que / quien) pintaste?

   d. Carlota, (que / quien) normalmente prefiere caminar, fue al trabajo en coche.

   e. Las tazas (que / quien) me mandó están rotas.

   f. El otoño es la estación (que / quien) me gusta más.

   g. Es el examen de inglés (que / quien) es muy difícil.

   h. La secretaria, para (que / quien) es este regalo, trabaja con mi madre.

   i. ¿Viste la pulsera (que / quien) acabo de poner en la mesa de noche?

   j. Mi padre, a (que / quien) le gusta mucho la historia, debe ser profesor.

2.   **Complete the sentences with a relative pronoun. Choose from the short list below. Some pronouns will be used more than once.** (1 pt. each)

   cuyo(a)(s)   lo que   que   quien(es)

   a. Deme el suéter _____ está sobre la cama.

   b. Ese hombre, _____ esposa es presidenta de esa compañía, es muy rico.

   c. Por favor, repite _____ acabas de decir.

   d. Los amigos de Geofredo, _____ vive lejos de aquí, visitan mañana.

   e. ¿Terminaste con _____ tenías que hacer?

   f. El chico, _____ padres nacieron en la Argentina, es de Chile.

   g. Los juguetes de Luisa, _____ los cuida bien, valen mucho.

   h. Estos médicos, _____ son famosos, asisten a una conferencia ahora.

   i. ¡Deme _____ quiero!

   j. Los niños, para _____ compramos la película, están en la sala ahora.

3.   **Combine each group of sentences into one sentence, joining each with the proper relative pronoun.**
(2 pts. each)

a.   Leo.
     Me gusta leer.
     _____

b.   Beto es el chico.
     Beto ganó la copa.
     _____

c.   Los primos Jorge y Josefa viajan a España.
     Ellos tienen diez años.
     _____

d.   Las manzanas son deliciosas.
     Compras las manzanas.
     _____

e.   La puerta no funciona.
     La puerta es reparada por su padre.
     _____

f.   La madre de Felipe es abogada.
     Ella trabaja mucho.
     _____

g.   Es una librería.
     Los precios son buenos.
     Vende muchos libros.
     _____

h.   El niño es sano.
     El niño se lava mucho.
     _____

i.   No sabía.
     Éste era el cuaderno.
     Querías el cuaderno.
     _____

j.   Es la cámara de Felipe.
     La cámara está rota.
     La cámara está con el técnico.
     _____

4. **Change these present indicative forms to the corresponding present subjunctive forms.** (1 pt. each)

a. es _____

b. cantamos _____

c. beben _____

d. muestro _____

e. piensa _____

f. ponemos _____

g. duermen _____

h. vuelve _____

i. tiene _____

j. conduces _____

k. trae _____

l. juegan _____

m. llegamos _____

n. busco _____

o. voy _____

p. sé _____

q. vienes _____

r. empiezan _____

s. damos _____

t. está _____

5. **Choose and circle the correct verb form to complete each sentence.** (2 pts. each)

a. Es dudoso que no (puedes / puedas) caminar durante dos semanas.

b. No está segura de lo que (necesita / necesite).

c. Es posible que (salen / salgan) muy temprano mañana.

d. No es verdad que (compro / compre) la muñeca.

e. ¿Quién es el hombre que (está / esté) sentado aquí?

f. No te preocupes. Les explico que no (comes / comas) el pescado.

g. Espero que todos (se divierten / se diviertan) bien.

h. Dudan que los periódicos no lo (imprimen / impriman).

i. No permito que (vas / vayas).

j. No hay duda que el equipo (gana / gane).

3

6.   **Translate the following into English.** (2 pts. each)

   a.   Ojalá que eso no se pase.

   _____

   b.   Le pedimos a ella que traiga las bebidas.

   _____

   c.   ¿Quién les aconseja a ellos que laven el suelo?

   _____

   d.   Es preferible que los jóvenes se pongan ropa formal para esta fiesta.

   _____

   e.   Recomiendo que no mires la televisión esta noche.

   _____

   f.   ¿Estás triste que Manolo no esté aquí?

   _____

   g.   Dudo que ella vaya a hacerlo.

   _____

   h.   Es importante que Uds. recuerden las formas del subjuntivo.

   _____

   i.   ¿Quieren tus padres que leas este libro?

   _____

   j.   Generalmente, no cree que estas historias sean verdaderas.

   _____

7.   **Translate the following into Spanish.** (2 pts. each)

   a.   It's good that (all of) you normally arrive on time.

   _____

   b.   His wife doesn't let (permit) him watch football every Sunday.

   _____

   c.   He suggests that I write the essay on the computer.

   _____

   d.   I'm telling you (tú) to stop!

   _____

   e.   Let's hope he's feeling better.

   _____

   f.   I don't like for you to walk home after the movie.

   _____

   g.   Do you (tú) want me to help you?

   _____

   h.   Tomás is happy that his sister is staying home tonight.

   _____

   i.   Many people prefer that their doctor be honest with them.

   _____

   j.   It is necessary for you (Ud.) to write that check today.

   _____

IV. THE SUBJUNCTIVE MOOD

Your knowledge of the formation of the imperative mood will make learning the forms of the present subjunctive easier for you.

SUBJUNCTIVE OF REGULAR VERBS

Do you remember the rule for the endings of negative commands?

> **Write that rule.**

4.1 _____

The notion of switching the endings (-*ar* to -*e*; -*er* and -*ir* to -*a*) applies to all forms of the present subjunctive. Study the forms of these regular infinitives.

trabajar (to work)

yo		nosotros	
	trabaj*e*		**trabaj*emos***
tú		vosotros	
	trabaj*es*		**trabaj*éis***
él		ellos	
ella	**trabaj*e***	ellas	**trabaj*en***
Ud.		Uds.	

esconder (to hide)

yo		nosotros	
	escond*a*		**escond*amos***
tú		vosotros	
	escond*as*		**escond*áis***
él		ellos	
ella	**escond*a***	ellas	**escond*an***
Ud.		Uds.	

vivir (to live)

yo		nosotros	
	viv*a*		**viv*amos***
tú		vosotros	
	viv*as*		**viv*áis***
él		ellos	
ella	**viv*a***	ellas	**viv*an***
Ud.		Uds.	

These forms should remind you of the imperative. However, there is no change for affirmative or negative verb forms.

 If these endings apply consistently, complete the charts below with the present subjunctive forms of the infinitives given. Model your responses on the previous examples.

4.2

1. **cambiar** (to change)

yo a.	nosotros d.
tú b.	vosotros **cambiéis**
él ella c. Ud.	ellos ellas e. Uds.

2. **comprender** (to understand)

yo a.	nosotros d.
tú b.	vosotros **comprendáis**
él ella c. Ud.	ellos ellas e. Uds.

3. **subir** (to go up, get on)

yo a.	nosotros d.
tú b.	vosotros **subáis**
él ella c. Ud.	ellos ellas e. Uds.

Write the correct present subjunctive form of each infinitive (in parentheses) in the spaces provided.

4.3   a.   Me gusta que (tú) _____ a tus padres cada mes. (visitar)

b.   Mis padres prefieren que sus hijos _____ su cuarto los viernes. (limpiar)

c.   Es importante que tú _____ en un buen vecindario. (vivir)

d. No queremos que ella _____ sus muebles; son antiguos y valen mucho. (vender)

e. El profesor está enojado de que Manolo no _____ su propia tarea. (escribir)

f. Es malo que ellos _____ la nueva familia. (burlarse de)

g. ¡Ojalá que todos nosotros _____ la lección! (comprender)

h. Deseo que Carmen y su novio _____ pronto. (casarse)

i. Te ruego que (tú) _____ la puerta. (abrir)

j. La madre recomienda que su hija _____ menos. (maquillarse)

SUBJUNCTIVE OF STEM-CHANGING VERBS

Great work! We will discuss how these forms translate a little later. For now, we will focus on the forms and apply these endings to stem-changing (shoe) verbs.

Stem-changing (shoe) verbs keep their changes in the present subjunctive throughout the singular (*yo, tú, él*) forms and the third person plural (*ellos*) form. The same subjunctive endings apply.

Let's look at **entender**.

 Answer the question.

4.4 What is the stem-change of this infinitive in the present indicative? _____

 Use that stem and the subjunctive endings (for -*er* infinitives) to build the forms of *entender* in the present subjunctive mood.

4.5   1. **entender** (to understand)

yo	nosotros
a.	d.
tú	vosotros
b.	**entendáis**
él	ellos
ella c.	ellas e.
Ud.	Uds.

Once you have completed all the forms, trace around all the stem-changing forms. You should draw that "shoe" shape that helps you remember that all but the *nosotros* and *vosotros* forms will also change in the subjunctive mood.

> **Make a list of at least five other *-er* stem-changing (shoe) verbs.**

4.6   a.   _____

      b.   _____

      c.   _____

      d.   _____

      e.   _____

      ✔ Adult check   _____

                                    Initial   Date

> **The same rules of formation apply to any stem-changing infinitive.**

> **Remembering that these are shoe verbs, write the present subjunctive forms of these infinitives.**

4.7   **encontrar** (to find)

yo a.	nosotros d.
tú b.	vosotros **encontréis**
él ella c. Ud.	ellos ellas e. Uds.

> **What are some other *-ar* shoe verbs you can think of? List at least five.**

4.8   a.   _____

      b.   _____

      c.   _____

      d.   _____

      e.   _____

      ✔ Adult check   _____

                                    Initial   Date

You have the -ir shoe verbs left to review. This group of infinitives has an added twist to its forms of the present subjunctive. Look closely at the subjunctive forms of **dormir** (to sleep).

dormir (to sleep)

yo **duerma**	nosotros **durmamos**
tú **duermas**	vosotros **durmáis**
él ella **duerma** Ud.	ellos ellas **duerman** Uds.

Trace around the stem-changing forms. You still have the shoe shape, but something else has changed.

Answer the following questions.

4.9   a. What is the additional change you have observed? _____

_____

b. Where have you seen this change before? _____

_____

Repeat this pattern for the following infinitive. Check to be sure you have made every necessary change.

4.10   **morir** (to die)

yo a.	nosotros d.
tú b.	vosotros **muráis**
él ella c. Ud.	ellos ellas e. Uds.

Answer the question.

4.11   In Exercise 4.7 you wrote the present subjunctive forms of *encontrar* ("to find"). Why didn't the *nosotros* and *vosotros* forms of *encontrar* have the *o* to *u* spelling change?

_____

_____

45

Continue with *-ir* shoe verbs in the present subjunctive. Search the forms of *pedir* ("to order, ask for") for its additional spelling change. Start by trying to draw the shoe around the stem-changing forms.

pedir (to order, ask for)

yo	nosotros
pida	pidamos
tú	vosotros
pidas	pidáis
él	ellos
ella pida	ellas pidan
Ud.	Uds.

 Answer the questions.

4.12   a.   If you attempted to draw the shoe, you would have found you couldn't. Why not?

_____

     b.   In the subjunctive mood, what additional spelling change occurs for *-ir* shoe verbs?

_____

YOU HAVE THREE RULES TO REMEMBER FOR FORMING THE PRESENT SUBJUNCTIVE:

■ Make the correct "shoe" change for the *yo, tú, él / ella / Ud.* and *ellos / ellas / Uds.* forms.

■ Write the correct subjunctive endings (which are, essentially, "flipped" from the present indicative).

■ Make the correct additional spelling change (*e–i* or *o–u*) for the *nosotros* and *vosotros* forms of those *-ir* verbs that have stem changes.

 Follow the same pattern to make the present subjunctive forms of *divertirse*.

4.13   **divertirse** (to have fun, enjoy oneself)

yo	nosotros
a.	d.
tú	vosotros
b.	**os divirtáis**
él	ellos
ella c.	ellas e.
Ud.	Uds.

SUBJUNCTIVE OF VERBS WITH SPELLING CHANGES

Within the regular verbs of the present subjunctive there is one more group of spelling-change infinitives. Your knowledge of tenses and moods such as the preterit and the imperative will help you learn this group easily.

 Study the present subjunctive forms of *pagar*. Answer the questions.

4.14 **pagar** (to pay)

yo		nosotros	
	pague		**paguemos**
tú		vosotros	
	pagues		**paguéis**
él		ellos	
ella	**pague**	ellas	**paguen**
Ud.		Uds.	

a. Apart from the subjunctive endings, how do these forms differ from their infinitive?

_____

b. Thinking back to the preterit tense, explain the reason for this spelling change.

_____

> As far as this spelling change is concerned, the difference between the present subjunctive and the preterit is that the *g* to *gu* changes only in the *yo* form of the preterit, but it runs through all the forms of the present subjunctive. (The "flipped" verb endings make it necessary.)

 Write the present subjunctive forms of the infinitive *jugar*. Remember, this infinitive is also a shoe verb!

4.15 **jugar** (to play)

yo	nosotros
a.	d.
tú)	vosotros
b.	**juguéis**
él	ellos
ella c.	ellas e.
Ud.	Uds.

47

There are three other kinds of infinitives in this category: those that end in *-zar*, *-car*, and *-ger*.

Answer the questions.

4.16 a. What spelling change must take place for verbs ending in *-zar*?_____

b. How are the forms of *-car* infinitives changed? _____

c. What spelling change occurs for verbs ending in *-ger*? _____

Put these rules to use by completing the present subjunctive forms of the following infinitives. Remember, the spelling changes occur in ALL forms.

4.17

1. **rezar** (to pray)

yo	nosotros
a.	d.
tú	vosotros
b.	**recéis**
él	ellos
ella c.	ellas e.
Ud.	Uds.

2. **chocarse (con)** (to crash into)

yo	nosotros
a.	d.
tú	vosotros
b.	**os choquéis**
él	ellos
ella c.	ellas e.
Ud.	Uds.

3. **escoger** (to choose)

yo	nosotros
a.	d.
tú	vosotros
b.	**escojáis**
él	ellos
ella c.	ellas e.
Ud.	Uds.

Write the *yo* and *nosotros* present subjunctive forms of each infinitive given.

4.18

		Yo	Nosotros
a.	buscar	_____	_____
b.	tragar	_____	_____
c.	empezar (e-ie)	_____	_____
d.	pagar	_____	_____
e.	escoger	_____	_____
f.	negar (e-ie)	_____	_____
g.	rogar (o-ue)	_____	_____
h.	tocar	_____	_____
i.	practicar	_____	_____
j.	llegar	_____	_____

The basic rule for forming any regular present subjunctive verb form is this:

> **The subjunctive stem comes from the *yo* form (without the *-o*) of the present indicative tense.**

What does this mean? It means that for REGULAR verb forms you should always consider the *yo* stem of the present tense. It also means that in the subjunctive mood you will have to consider many stem and spelling changes.

For example:

> **If you are conjugating the infinitive *tener* in the subjunctive mood, and you are working off the *yo* stem of the present indicative tense, *teng-* is your new stem (remember to drop the *-o*). You will use this stem (*teng-*) for ALL the forms of the present subjunctive.**

Understanding these rules isn't difficult, especially if you can remember the stem-change or spelling-change for every *yo* form.

Answer the following questions.

4.19   a. What are the guidelines for subjunctive endings?_____

_____

_____

b. What three rules do you have to remember for forming the present subjunctive?

1. _____

2. _____

3. _____

Write the correct present subjunctive forms for *tener* in the box below.

4.20   **tener** (to have)

yo	nosotros
a.	d.
tú	vosotros
b.	**tengáis**
él	ellos
ella c.	ellas e.
Ud.	Uds.

Make a list of ten infinitives whose *yo* forms have a spelling change in the present indicative tense. Write the *yo* form next to each verb.

               Infinitive   Yo

4.21   a.   _____   –   _____

b.   _____   –   _____

c.   _____   –   _____

d.   _____   –   _____

e.   _____   –   _____

f.   _____   –   _____

g.   _____   –   _____

h.   _____   –   _____

i.   _____   –   _____

j.   _____   –   _____

> **Change these forms of the present indicative tense to the *yo* and *Uds.* forms of the present subjunctive.**

4.22   Yo   Uds.

a.   pongo   _____   _____

b.   digo   _____   _____

c.   traigo   _____   _____

d.   salgo   _____   _____

e.   escojo   _____   _____

f.   conduzco   _____   _____

g.   hago   _____   _____

h.   aparezco   _____   _____

i.   tuerzo   _____   _____

j.   caigo   _____   _____

VOCABULARIO

estar cansado(a) – *to be tired*

estar enojado(a) – *to be angry*

estar contento(a) – *to be content, happy*

estar alegre – *to be happy*

estar tranquilo(a) – *to be calm*

estar encantado(a) – *to be enchanted, delighted*

estar emocionado(a) – *to be excited*

estar deprimido(a) – *to be depressed*

estar enamorado(a) – *to be in love*

estar enfermo(a) – *to be sick*

estar ocupado(a) – *to be busy*

estar orgulloso(a) – *to be proud*

estar preocupado(a) – *to be worried*

estar desilusionado(a) – *to be disillusioned, disappointed*

estar triste – *to be sad*

estar de buen/mal humor – *to be in a good/bad mood*

SUBJUNCTIVE OF IRREGULAR VERBS

Fortunately, there aren't many irregular stems in the present subjunctive tense. Memorize the following forms.

ir (to go)

yo		nosotros	
	vaya		**vayamos**
tú		vosotros	
	vayas		**vayáis**
él		ellos	
ella	**vaya**	ellas	**vayan**
Ud.		Uds.	

ser (to be)

yo		nosotros	
	sea		**seamos**
tú		vosotros	
	seas		**seáis**
él		ellos	
ella	**sea**	ellas	**sean**
Ud.		Uds.	

dar (to give)

yo		nosotros	
	dé		**demos**
tú		vosotros	
	des		**deis**
él		ellos	
ella	**dé**	ellas	**den**
Ud.		Uds.	

estar (to be)

yo		nosotros	
	esté		**estemos**
tú		vosotros	
	estés		**estéis**
él		ellos	
ella	**esté**	ellas	**estén**
Ud.		Uds.	

saber (to know)

yo		nosotros	
	sepa		**sepamos**
tú		vosotros	
	sepas		**sepáis**
él		ellos	
ella	**sepa**	ellas	**sepan**
Ud.		Uds.	

➤ **Compare the present indicative and the present subjunctive forms of irregular verbs by changing these present indicative forms to their equivalent in the present subjunctive.**

4.23   a.   van   _____

b.   sé   _____

c.   están   _____

d.   doy   _____

e.   sabemos _____

f.   son   _____

g.   eres   _____

h.   vas   _____

i.   estamos _____

j.   soy   _____

k. voy _____

l. sabes _____

m. estoy _____

n. es _____

o. vamos _____

We often judge the actions of others and have preferences regarding how others should act. Use the present indicative form of *preferir* and the present subjunctive form of the infinitive in parentheses to state each person's preference. Follow the example.

Example: Yo (hacer buen tiempo).
Prefiero que haga buen tiempo.

4.24 a. Mi amigo (nosotros/ir al cine el sábado).

_____

_____

b. Mi hermana (yo/no ser impaciente con ella).

_____

_____

c. El jefe (los empleados/no ir a casa temprano).

_____

_____

d. Yo (mi hija/ver una película interesante).

_____

_____

e. Nosotros (los jóvenes/estar juntos para la cena).

_____

_____

f. Los padres (su hijo/darse cuenta del valor de la educación).

_____

_____

g. Tu abuela (tú/saber la genealogía de la familia).

_____

_____

h. Papá (yo/darle cinco dólares a mi hermano).

_____

_____

i.   Los profesores (nosotros/ser estudiosos).

_____

_____

j.   La Sra. de Burgos (su esposo/saber la fecha del aniversario).

_____

_____

OPTIONAL ACTIVITY C: Using phrases from the vocabulary list in this section, write ten sentences using the subjunctive.

Examples: El abuelo prefiere que los nietos vengan mañana.
          La madre prefiere que su hijo corte el césped esta tarde.

a.   _____

b.   _____

c.   _____

d.   _____

e.   _____

f.   _____

g.   _____

h.   _____

i.   _____

j.   _____

Exercise 1. Listen for the present subjunctive verb form in each sentence. Write the form you hear in the space provided. [CD–F, Track 6]

a. _____

b. _____

c. _____

d. _____

e. _____

f. _____

g. _____

h. _____

i. _____

j. _____

Exercise 2. Change each infinitive to the *él* form of the present subjunctive. [CD–F, Track 7]

a. _____

b. _____

c. _____

d. _____

e. _____

f. _____

g. _____

h. _____

i. _____

j. _____

Exercise 3. Listen to each sentence carefully. Choose and circle the correct English translation of each sentence you hear. [CD–F, Track 8]

1. a. I prefer to come at 8:00.
   b. You prefer that I come at 8:00.
   c. I prefer that you come at 8:00.

2. a. We hope she plays well.
   b. We hope to play well.
   c. She hopes we play well.

3. a. It's important to go to the doctor's office.
   b. It's important that we go to the doctor's office.
   c. It's important that they go to the doctor's office.

4. a. You don't believe that I'm telling the truth.
   b. I don't believe that you're telling the truth.
   c. I don't believe in telling the truth.

5. a. It's good to cook a good dinner.
   b. It's good that you're cooking a good dinner.
   c. You're good at cooking a good dinner.

6. a. You wish to return our key.
   b. We wish to return your key.
   c. We wish you would return our key.

7. a. You're irritated that he's making so much noise.
   b. He's irritated that you're making so much noise.
   c. It's irritating to make so much noise.

8. a. He doubts that I can do it.
   b. I doubt that he can do it.
   c. I doubt that they can do it.

9. a. They beg you to clean the room.
   b. You beg them to clean the room.
   c. He begs them to clean the room.

10. a. I'm happy they don't have a fever now.
    b. I'm happy not to have a fever now.
    c. They're happy that I don't have a fever now.

✔ Adult check _____
                        Initial   Date

 Review the material in this section in preparation for the Self Test. This Self Test will check your mastery of this particular section as well as your knowledge of the previous sections.

SELF TEST 4

4.01   **Circle the present subjunctive form in each group.** (1 pt. each)

a.   alcance   alcancé   alcanzaré

b.   juegues   jugué   juegas

c.   pierden   pierdan   perdieron

d.   fui   vaya   voy

e.   tiene   tengas   tengo

f.   digo   dé   di

g.   duerman   duermen   dormirán

h.   gusta   gustan   guste

i.   subiría   subió   suba

j.   cuentes   cuentas   conté

4.02   **For each group, change the infinitives to the form of the present subjunctive that agrees with the subject given.** (1 pt. each blank)

a.   la familia

   participar _____

   vestirse _____

   perder _____

b.   tus amigos

   caerse   _____

   abrir _____

   ayudar _____

c.   la estudiante y yo

   salir _____

   estudiar _____

   conocerse _____

d.   Héctor y Ud.

   solicitar _____

   divertirse _____

   comer _____

e. yo

    preferir _____

    poner _____

    brincar _____

f. tú

    subir _____

    conducir _____

    devolver _____

g. tu amigo y yo

    empezar _____

    sentarse _____

    vivir _____

h. el camarero

    leer _____

    ver _____

    estar _____

i. las máquinas

    encender _____

    apagar _____

    funcionar _____

j. tú

    desayunar _____

    ser _____

    huir _____

4.03   **Change the present indicative tense forms to the corresponding forms in the present subjunctive.**
(1 pt. each)

a. sacan _____

b. paseas _____

c. me quedo _____

d. salimos _____

e. alza _____

f. tienes _____

g. ven _____

h. voy _____

i. creemos _____

j. piensa _____

k. quiero _____

l. eres _____

m. escriben _____

n. doy _____

o. jugamos _____

4.04 **Complete each sentence with a present subjunctive form of a verb that makes sense, according to the cue.** (1 pt. each)

a. Manolo ayuda a limpiar la casa.

   La madre exige qué Manolo _____ el polvo.

b. El perro tiene hambre.

   Es bueno que Juan le _____ de comer al perro.

c. Tú tienes sueño.

   Es necesario que tú _____ temprano.

d. Las muchachas son muy bonitas.

   No es necesario que ellas _____ .

e. Elena tuvo un accidente.

   Es malo que Elena _____ herida.

f. La secretaria tiene mucho trabajo.

   El trabajo requiere que la secretaria _____ los documentos importantes.

g. La familia Gómez va a España.

   Es importante que la familia Gómez _____ el equipaje.

h. Alonso no tiene mucho dinero.

   No es justo que Alonso _____ la cena de todos.

i. Pedro va al hospital para visitar a su madre.

   Es bueno que Pedro le _____ flores a su mamá.

j. Hace viento y está lloviendo.

   Es muy importante que tú _____ la puerta.

4.05   **Answer the questions in complete Spanish sentences.** (2 pts. each)

a.   ¿Es importante que estudies?

    _____

b.   ¿Es necesario que tu madre cocine para ti?

    _____

c.   ¿Es malo que un amigo diga una mentira?

    _____

d.   ¿Es necesario que una persona gane un sueldo grande?

    _____

e.   ¿Es preferible que te bañes todos los días?

    _____

f.   ¿Es dudoso que existan los marcianos (Martians)?

    _____

g.   ¿Es poco probable que seas presidente algún día?

    _____

h.   ¿Es bueno que termines la tarea?

    _____

i.   ¿Es necesario que obedezcas las leyes?

    _____

j.   ¿Es raro que asisten Uds. a una obra de teatro?

    _____

V. USES OF THE SUBJUNCTIVE

You have already begun to write subjunctive sentences as practice for formation of those forms. Have you noticed that the sentences are all of the same structure? They are often written as a main (indicative) clause joined to a dependent (subjunctive) clause with the relative pronoun *que*. Think of it as a kind of equation:

main (indicative) clause + *que* + dependent (subjunctive) clause

This is not the only way to use the subjunctive, but it's where our lesson begins.

Practice this sentence structure. Complete the sentences by writing the most logical form and mood of the appropriate infinitive.

5.1 a. El profesor _____ que los estudiantes _____ la tarea. (exigir / hacer)

b. (It) _____ bueno que tú lo _____ bien. (ser / comprender)

c. Los padres _____ que el bebé _____ de buen humor. (desear / estar)

d. La abuelita _____ emocionada de que Elena _____ este verano. (estar / casarse)

e. Yo _____ que mi amiga _____ a la función conmigo. (pedir / asistir)

f. Los estudiantes _____ que Pepe _____ el diccionario. (dudar / traer)

g. Muchos niños _____ que su papá _____ miedo. (no creer / tener)

h. Yo _____ que Uds. _____ venir con nosotros. (esperar / poder)

i. Consuelo _____ furiosa que su novio le _____ tales cosas. (ponerse / decir)

j. (It) _____ necesario que tú le _____ pronto a tu madre. (ser / escribir)

Arrange the words logically in order to complete the sentences. Remember the correct word order. The first one has been done for you.

main (indicative) clause + *que* + dependent (subjunctive) clause

5.2 a. (que / importante / haga / es) los ejercicios.

Es importante que haga los ejercicios.

b. (me gusta / visiten / que) el domingo.

_____

c. (estés / que / siento) enfermo.

_____

d. (que / queremos / participen) en la clase de inglés.

_____

61

e.   (dudoso / veamos / que / es) el avión pronto.

_____

f.   (llene / necesario / es / que) la solicitud.

_____

g.   (niegan / vayan / que) al cine por la noche.

_____

h.   (se quiten / prefiere / que) los zapatos.

_____

i.   (que / no se permite / lo pongas) allí.

_____

j.   (bueno / es / le cuide / que) bien.

_____

_____

✔ Adult check _____
                        Initial   Date

Often, a Spanish subjunctive sentence is translated using *to* in English. For example:

Yo quiero que escribas la carta. *I want you to write the letter.*

The sentence could be translated as *I want that you may (might) write the letter.* The subjunctive verb form most literally translates as *may* or *might*. The most natural translation for English speakers, however, is the *to* translation.

Here is another sample.

Nosotros pedimos que ella venga con nosotros.

The literal translation is *We ask that she may (might) come with us.* The most natural English translation is *We ask her to come with us.*

Translate each sentence into English, using the most natural translation.

5.3 a.   Prefieres que Beto no hable más.

   _____

   b.   Es importante que no gastes demasiado dinero hoy.

   _____

   c.   Estoy contento de que pienses volver temprano.

   _____

   d.   Necesito que vayas a la tienda ahora.

   _____

   e.   Esperamos que ella se sienta mejor pronto.

   _____

You may remember that you studied the infinitive construction earlier. Why could you use it then and not now? Here are the rules:

■ Use the *infinitive* construction when the subject of the main clause is the *same* as the subject of the subordinate clause:

Los niños quieren comer helado. *The children want to eat ice cream.*
This sentence describes the *children's* desire for *their* eating ice cream.
The subject of both actions is the same.

■ Use the *infinitive* construction when making *generalized statements*.

Es bueno tener amigos. *It's good to have friends.*
Who has friends? No one in particular. This is a general statement.

■ Use the *subjunctive* when the subject of the main clause (requiring subjunctive) is *different* from the subject of the subordinate clause.

Queremos que Elena juegue bien. *We want Elena to play well.*
This sentence tells how *we* want *Elena* to play.
The subjects of these two actions are different.

■ Use the *subjunctive* when one is making evaluative statements about a specific person's actions.

Es bueno que Pepe tenga muchos amigos. *It's good that Pepe has many friends.*
This sentence makes a judgement about Pepe, specifically.

Study the ways to determine if a sentence requires an infinitive or a subjunctive construction.

1. An infinitive construction makes a general statement.

2. An infinitive construction makes a statement about the actions of the subject of the main clause.

3. A sentence requires a subjunctive construction when someone makes a judgment about someone else.

4. A subjunctive statement is specific rather than general.

5. A subjunctive statement will normally have a different subject for the main clause and the subordinate clause.

Mark the subjunctive sentence with an *S*. Mark the infinitive sentence with an *I*.

5.4   a.   _____   I don't want to wash dishes.

           _____   I want my brother to wash the dishes.

      b.   _____   She wants to get better.

           _____   She wants you to get better.

      c.   _____   We need you to turn on the lights.

           _____   We need to turn on the lights.

      d.   _____   They like to take a walk at night.

           _____   They like for me to take a walk at night.

      e.   _____   Is it necessary for you to talk so loudly?

           _____   Is it necessary to talk so loudly?

      f.   _____   It's good to greet people politely.

           _____   It's good that your son greets people politely.

      g.   _____   He denies that she saw him that night.

           _____   He denies seeing anything that night.

      h.   _____   Why don't they allow parking here?

           _____   Why don't they allow me to park here?

      i.   _____   We hope to be lucky.

           _____   We hope she's lucky.

      j.   _____   I insist they use good manners.

           _____   I insist on using good manners.

Using the example as a model, translate each of the sentences. Use the correct subjunctive forms.

5.5 a. *You hope that they (may, might) help.* **Esperas que ayuden.**

We hope that she helps. _____

They hope that I help. _____

b. *We doubt that they can stand it.* **Dudamos que puedan aguantarlo.**

You (friendly) doubt that I can stand it. _____

(All of) you doubt that they can stand it. _____

c. *We prefer that you not dress in such a way.* **Preferimos que Ud. no se vista de tal manera.**

I prefer that my boyfriend not dress in such a way. _____

_____

They prefer that their granddaughter not dress in such a way. _____

_____

d. *I'm asking you to be quiet.* **Te pido que te calles.**

We're asking you (formal) to be quiet. _____

You're (friendly) asking them to be quiet. _____

e. *I don't let (permit) you smoke.* **No permito que fumes.**

They don't let me smoke._____

We don't let them smoke. _____

f. *I advise you to watch that program.* **Te aconsejo que mires ese programa.**

She advises him to watch that program. _____

My friends advise us to watch that program. _____

_____

g. *I want you to stop.* **Quiero que te pares.**

We want him to stop. _____

She wants me to stop. _____

h. *You're sad that it's raining.* **Estás triste que llueva.**

We are sad that it's raining. _____

They are sad that it's raining. _____

65

At this point, we need to discuss what kinds of clauses require the subjunctive. Like any other verb tense or mood, there are rules to determine when it may be appropriate to use it.

> The following main clauses require the subjunctive when the subjects are different:
>
> - Expressions of emotion
> - Expressions of wish and desire
> - Expressions of request
> - Expressions of doubt or denial
> - Impersonal expressions

Let's study these uses of the subjunctive one by one.

EXPRESSIONS OF EMOTION

> **Estoy contenta de que me traigas un regalo.**
> I'm happy that you are bringing me a present.

 Answer the following questions.

5.6   a.   What is the main clause of the above sentence? _____

       b.   Is this sentence really about my happiness or about bringing a gift? _____

Because the sentence is really evaluating *bringing*, judging it as causing happiness, the subjunctive is required for *traer*.

Here is another example:

> **Te sientes irritada de que haga tanto calor.**
> You're irritated that it's so hot.

       c.   Explain why *haga* is in the subjunctive: _____

_____

_____

> Here are some other expressions of emotion:
>
> **estar (contento, triste, emocionado, etc.) de que** – to be (happy, sad, excited, etc.) that…
>
> **sentir que** – to be sorry that, to regret that…
>
> **darle vergüenza que** – to be ashamed that…
>
> **tener miedo de que (temer que)** – to be afraid (to fear) that…
>
> **sorprenderse de que** – to be surprised that…

66

Put the infinitives into the appropriate Spanish present subjunctive form.

5.7   a. Manolo no estudia para su examen de español.

Su madre no está contenta que Manolo no _____ (estudiar) para su examen de español.

b. A Mariela no le gustan las motocicletas.

A Mariela no le gusta que Pepito _____ (conducir) una motocicleta.

c. Jorge necesita trabajar en el jardín.

Su madre está contenta que Jorge _____ (cortar) el césped pronto.

d. La madre no sabe donde están sus hijos.

La madre tiene miedo que sus hijos no _____ (estar) seguros.

e. Las hijas son muy inteligentes.

Los padres están emocionados que sus hijas _____ (terminar) sus estudios este año.

f. El niño está en el techo del garaje.

La madre teme que su niño _____ (caerse).

g. La niña hace la cama.

La madre se sorprende de que su niña _____ (hacer) la cama.

h. Tenemos que mudarnos a otra ciudad.

Luisa está triste que (nosotros) _____ (mudarse) a otra ciudad.

i. No estás contenta aquí.

Siento que (tú) no _____ (estar) contenta aquí.

j. Mis padres no se portan bien en la fiesta.

Me da vergüenza que mis padres no _____ (portarse) bien en la fiesta.

Adult check _____

Initial   Date

EXPRESSIONS OF WISH AND DESIRE

Study and consider the following translated sentence.

> **Mi mamá quiere que yo limpie mi cuarto.**
> My mom wants me to clean my room.

Just because your mother wants you to do so, does that necessarily mean (all the time) that you will clean your room? *No.*

Because we can't be sure that *yo* will clean the room, *limpie* is in the subjunctive. The sentence is really about *mamá wanting* the room cleaned.

Here are some common expressions of wish and desire:

> **desear que** – to wish that
>
> **querer que** – to want that
>
> **preferir que** – to prefer that
>
> **esperar que** – to hope that

Any of these phrases may be used in the negative and still require the subjunctive.

> **Deseo que salgas bien en el examen.**
> I want you to do well on the exam.
> **No deseo que salgas mal en el examen.**
> I don't want you to do poorly on the exam.

Use the expression *querer que* **("to want that"), the subjunctive mood of the infinitives given, and the cues provided to describe what each person wants to happen. Use the cues and your knowledge of Spanish to complete the sentences.**

5.8   a.   Manolo necesita ayuda. (la profesora / ayudar)

Manolo _____

b.   La cocina está muy sucia. (nosotros / limpiar)

Mamá _____

c.   El bebé tiene hambre. (alguien / dar)

El bebé _____

d.   Un hombre acaba de robar la tienda. (el ladrón / escaparse)

La policía _____

e.   Yo tengo un libro de la biblioteca. (Mamá / devolver)

Yo _____

Read each sentence and question. Then write an appropriate answer in Spanish, using a subjunctive expression. Use the cues in parentheses to form your answer.

5.9   **Example:**   A Manolo le gusta jugar al fútbol.
                    ¿Qué desea para el campeonato?

   a.   de su equipo; (jugar bien) **Desea que su equipo juegue bien.**
   b.   de sus amigos; (venir al partido) **Desea que sus amigos vengan al partido.**
   c.   del árbitro; (tener razón) **Desea que el árbitro tenga razón.**
   d.   del entrenador; (no estar enojado) **Desea que el entrenador no esté enojado.**
   e.   de sus padres; (tener orgullo) **Desea que sus padres tengan orgullo.**

1.   María va a cumplir diez años.
    ¿Qué quiere recibir para el cumpleaños?

   a.   de sus padres; (una bicicleta)_____

   b.   de sus abuelos; (un cheque) _____

   c.   de su primo; (una cámara) _____

   d.   de su tío; (discos) _____

   e.   de Ana; (un suéter) _____

2.   Anita se va a graduar esta noche.
    ¿Qué espera para la noche tan importante?

   a.   de Mariana; (le dar un regalo)_____

   b.   de sus profesores; (le dar buenas notas) _____

   c.   de sus padres; (estar contentos)_____

   d.   de su hermano; (no tener celos)_____

   e.   de los niños; (portarse bien)_____

3.   Carlos va a un trabajo nuevo.
    ¿Qué quiere el primer día del trabajo?

   a.   de la recepcionista; (decirle «Buenos días») _____

   b.   de Tomás; (trabajar juntos) _____

   c.   de su jefe; (darle un escritorio grande)_____

   d.   de sus padres; (regalarle un traje nuevo)_____

   e.   de su hermana; (venir a almorzar con él) _____

Adult check _____
                              Initial   Date

EXPRESSIONS OF REQUEST

Here are some common expressions of request:

> **sugerir (e-ie) que** – to suggest that
>
> **mandar que** – to order that
>
> **pedir (e-i) que** – to ask that
>
> **rogar (o-ue) que** – to beg that
>
> **aconsejar que** – to advise that
>
> **recomendar (e-ie) que** – to recommend that

These phrases may also be used negatively in subjunctive sentences.

Answer the following questions in Spanish. Use a subjunctive expression in each answer. The first one has been done for you.

5.10 a. Carlos conduce delante de una escuela. ¿Cómo debe conducir?

Sugiero que Carlos conduzca lentamente.

b. Guillermo tiene una reunión importante. Está cansado. ¿Qué le pides?

c. Laura le dijo una mentira a su mamá, pero su mamá ya lo sabe. ¿Qué le aconsejas a Laura?

d. Alberto tiene una fiebre muy alta. No puede trabajar hoy. ¿Qué le recomiendas?

e. Los pantalones del Sr. Garza no le quedan bien. Están apretados. ¿Qué le sugieres?

f. Tu hija está enferma. Hace cinco días que no asiste a las clases. Se siente sola. ¿Qué le pides a ella?

g. Tu tío no puede respirar profundamente. ¿Qué le sugieres?

h. Ángel no tiene suficiente dinero para comprar su disco compacto favorito. ¿Qué le aconsejas?

i. Ramón y tú están en el camino a la fiesta de cumpleaños de tu primo. Están perdidos. No tienen mapa y la fiesta empieza en cinco minutos. ¿Qué le sugieres a Ramón?

j. El equipo participa en un campeonato de fútbol. Hace tres días que no juega bien. ¿Qué le pides al equipo?

EXPRESSIONS OF DOUBT OR DENIAL

Anytime one casts doubt on or expresses disbelief in an action or forbids or denies the performance of an action, the subjunctive is needed for that action.

> **Dudo que tengas razón.**
> I doubt that you're right.
>
> **No crees que ella lo pueda hacer.**
> You don't think that she can do it (that she may be able to do it).
>
> **No se permite que hablemos durante el examen.**
> We're not permitted to talk during the test. (It's not permitted that we talk during the test.)

> **dudar que** – to doubt that
>
> **es dudoso que** – it's doubtful that
>
> **no creer que** – not to believe that
>
> **negar (e-ie) que** – to deny that
>
> **no permitir que** – not to allow (permit) that
>
> **no es cierto que** – it's not certain that
>
> **no estar seguro de que** – not to be sure that
>
> **no creer que** – not to believe that
>
> **no pensar que** – not to think that

Be careful with these phrases. Making them negative or affirmative can change whether or not you are expressing doubt. Use the indicative if there is no doubt or denial. Translate and compare the first two statements.

5.11   a.   Dudas que él **venga** a tiempo._____

b.   No dudas que él **viene** a tiempo.   _____

c.   Once you write *no* in front of *dudar*, is that phrase any longer an expression of doubt? _____

d.   Why? _____

e.   Why is the subjunctive unnecessary in the second example? _____

_____

> **Think of it this way: No doubt, no denial, no subjunctive.**

> Determine if these English sentences would need the subjunctive. Write *S* for each subjunctive sentence or *I* for each indicative sentence in the space provided.

5.12   a. _____ I know you can hear me.

b. _____ She doubts they'll be able to go.

c. _____ Do you deny that he said that?

d. _____ I doubt it could happen here.

e. _____ He doesn't think that it's too expensive.

f. _____ We don't doubt that you can do it.

g. _____ We know they're telling us the truth.

h. _____ You don't believe he came home on time.

i. _____ It's doubtful that it will rain.

j. _____ It's unlikely he'll call.

Complete the sentences with the opposite meaning. Use the subjunctive where necessary. The first one has been done for you.

5.13   a.   No dudo que pueden oírnos, pero Lupe *duda que puedan oírnos* _____ .

b.   No niegas que salen pronto, pero yo _____ .

c.   Yo creo que viene aquí, pero ellos _____ .

d.   Nosotros creemos que es mejor, pero tú _____ .

e.   No niego que se viste mal, pero su esposa _____ .

f.   Ellos no dudan que funciona bien, pero Papá _____ .

g.   Ella cree que yo lo siento, pero mis amigos _____ .

h.   Ricardo está seguro de que terminamos los estudios este año, pero mi hermana _____

_____ .

i.   Yo creo que te gradúas, pero Juan _____ .

j.   Para mí, es cierto que nieva pronto, pero para ti, _____ .

IMPERSONAL EXPRESSIONS

Impersonal expressions that are the equivalent of implied commands or judgments must be followed by the subjunctive.

> **(no) es importante que** – it's (not) important that
>
> **(no) es preciso que** – it's (not) necessary that
>
> **(no) es necesario que** – it's (not) necessary that
>
> **(no) es bueno (malo) que** – it's (not) good (bad) that
>
> **(no) es posible (imposible) que** – it's (not) possible (impossible) that
>
> **ojalá que** – let's hope that / May God grant that

If you are making a **general statement of importance, morality,** etc., you may use the **infinitive**.

> **Es bueno contribuir a las organizaciones benéficas.**
> It's good to contribute to charities.

If you are **evaluating the actions of a specific person(s)**, use the **subjunctive** after the impersonal expression.

> **Es bueno que tú contribuyas a las organizaciones benéficas.**
> It's good that you contribute to charities.

Translate the pairs. Be mindful of which requires the subjunctive and which needs the infinitive.

5.14 a. It's important to be courteous. _____

_____

It's important for young people to be courteous. _____

_____

b. Is it necessary for me to pack a suitcase? _____

_____

Is it necessary to pack a suitcase? _____

_____

c. It's not good that we're failing the class. _____

_____

It's not good to fail the class. _____

_____

d. It's impossible for Nicolás to leave at 5:00. _____

_____

It's impossible to leave at 5:00. _____

_____

e. It's not necessary to take antibiotics for the flu. _____

_____

It's not necessary for your child to take antibiotics for the flu. _____

_____

Judge what's going on in each picture. Use a variety of impersonal expressions followed by a subjunctive phrase to describe your thoughts.

5.15

a. _____   b. _____

_____   _____

c. _____

d. _____

_____

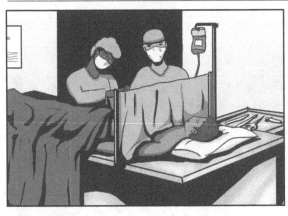

e. _____

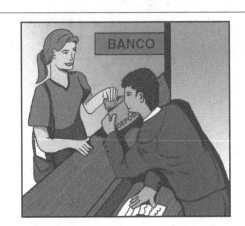

f. _____

_____

g. _____

h. _____

i. _____

_____

j. _____

_____

 LISTENING EXERCISES V

Exercise 1. Listen to each of the following clauses. Decide which dependent clause completes the sentences you hear. Circle your choice. [CD–F, Track 9]

1. a. puede levantar cien kilos.

    b. pueda levantar cien kilos.

    c. poder levantar cien kilos.

2. a. tengan cuidado.

    b. tienen cuidado.

    c. tener cuidado.

3. a. portarse bien.

    b. se porten bien.

    c. se portan bien.

4. a. el coche funciona bien.

    b. el coche funcione bien

    c. el coche funcionó bien.

5. a. estás resfriado.

    b. estar resfriado.

    c. estés resfriado.

6. a. tu papá conduce.

    b. tu papá conduzca.

    c. tu papá esté conduciendo.

7. a. voy con ellos.

    b. ir con ellos.

    c. vaya con ellos.

8. a. están sentados se llama Raúl.

    b. está sentado se llama Raúl.

    c. estén sentados se llama Raúl.

9. a. mi esposo obtiene un puesto nuevo.

    b. mi esposo obtenga un puesto nuevo.

    c. mi esposo obtuvo un puesto nuevo.

10. a. no sea verdad.

    b. no es verdad.

    c. no ser verdad.

Exercise 2. Translate the sentences you hear into English. [CD–F, Track 10]

a. _____

b. _____

c. _____

d. _____

e. _____

f. _____

g. _____

h. _____

i. _____

j. _____

✔ Adult check _____

Initial   Date

 Review the material in this section in preparation for the Self Test. This Self Test will check your mastery of this particular section as well as your knowledge of the previous sections.

SELF TEST 5

5.01   **Write the correct subjunctive form of each infinitive given.** (1 pt. each)

a. escribir (el jefe) _____

b. comenzar (los amigos) _____

c. caerse (yo) _____

d. irse (Paco y yo) _____

e. querer (tú) _____

f. llegar (Uds.) _____

g. rezar (los esclavos) _____

h. no decir (la Sra. Gutierrez) _____

i. encontrar (mucha gente) _____

j. pasar (nosotros) _____

5.02   **Change these present indicative forms to the corresponding subjunctive forms.** (1 pt. each)

a. dan _____

b. buscamos _____

c. pone _____

d. pides _____

e. salimos _____

f. tiene _____

g. comprendes _____

h. vuelves _____

i. es _____

j. se acuestan _____

5.03   **Unscramble the following sentences to make logical subjunctive statements or questions.** (2 pts. each)

a.   no eches / que / el balón / prefiero

_____

b.   no creen / el mundo / que / sea redondo

_____

c.   ocurra / que / es / imposible / eso / ahora

_____

d.   pido / conmigo / que / vengas / te

_____

e.   con los quehaceres / piden / nos / que / ayudemos / nuestros padres

_____

f.   llamen / no permite / después de las nueve / que / de la noche / por teléfono

_____

g.   para mí / que / lo hagas / quiero

_____

h.   desilusionada / que / está / de / se diviertan / no

_____

i.   ¿no / arregle / que / el coche / dudas?

_____

j.   que / asistan / a la reunión / ojalá / todos

_____

5.04   **Change the infinitives in parentheses to the correct mood (present indicative or present subjunctive) and the correct form. Be careful! Not every sentence will require the subjunctive!** (2 pts. each)

   a.   Yo (querer) que Ud. me (dejar) en paz.

        Yo _____ que Ud. me _____ en paz.

   b.   (ser) preferible que los estudiantes no (escribir) en los pupitres.

        _____ preferible que los estudiantes no _____ en los pupitres.

   c.   El editor (pedir) que la compañía no (imprimir) el artículo.

        El editor _____ que la compañía no _____ el artículo.

   d.   Los padres les (aconsejar) a sus niños que (ahorrar) el dinero.

        Los padres les _____ a sus niños que _____ el dinero.

   e.   A Teresa no le (gustar) que Guillermo (charlar) con otras chicas.

        A Teresa no le _____ que Guillermo _____ con otras chicas.

   f.   Yo (estar) seguro de que el profesor (tener) razón.

        Yo _____ seguro de que el profesor _____ razón.

   g.   (ser) necesario que Hilda (saber) el número de teléfono.

        _____ necesario que Hilda _____ el número de teléfono.

   h.   Jorge (pedir) que Juana (ir) al cine con él.

        Jorge _____ que Juana _____ al cine con él.

   i.   Yo (negar) que tal lugar (existir)

        Yo _____ que tal lugar _____ .

   j.   Uds. (creer) que la iglesia (estar) cerca.

        Uds. _____ que la iglesia _____ cerca.

5.05   **Translate the following sentences into Spanish.** (2 pts. each)

   a.   I hope you (tú) feel better tomorrow.

        _____

   b.   She wants us to show the homework to her.

        _____

   c.   Who recommends that they eat more fruit?

        _____

   d.   He's telling us not to write with a pencil.

        _____

   e.   Don't you (tú) want me to hear the story?

        _____

   f.   It's important for Marcos to set the table.

        _____

g. Let's hope their friends don't read the letter.

_____

h. We don't want you (Ud.) to give the money to him!

_____

i. Susana doesn't think that Jorge is at home now.

_____

j. I believe he's a good man.

_____

64 / 80	Score _____
	Adult check _____
	Initial Date

Before you take the LIFEPAC Test, you may want to do one or more of these self checks.

1. _____ Read the objectives. Determine if you can do them.

2. _____ Restudy the material related to any objectives that you cannot do.

3. _____ Use the SQ3R study procedure to review the material.

4. _____ Review all activities, Self Tests, and LIFEPAC vocabulary words.

5. _____ Restudy areas of weakness indicated by the last Self Test.

VI. CULTURAL INVESTIGATION

Explore the culture of a Spanish-speaking country. Complete a paper, using the following resources.

Part I   **Use an atlas.**

    A. Locate your country on a world map.

    B. Create a full-color map of your country and find the following details about your country.

        1. the capital city

        2. three other major cities

        3. any mountain ranges

        4. any major river systems or lakes

        5. all neighboring countries

Part II   **Use an encyclopedia (electronic or printed).**

    A. Identify the current system of government.

    B. Identify the chief leader's name and title (king, dictator, etc.).

    C. Identify any governing bodies or houses (parliament, congress, etc.).

    D. Describe the electoral process, in brief (popular vote, hereditary ascension, etc.).

    E. Frequency of elections, if any.

Part III   **Use an almanac.**

    A. Identify your country's most important exports.

    B. Identify your country's per capita income.

    C. Does your country utilize or export any natural resources?

    D. Identify how many years of mandatory schooling each citizen should have.

Part IV   **Use the following website: www.cia.gov**

Click on *The World Fact Book*, scroll through the information, and identify the following:

    A. total population

    B. infant mortality

    C. average life expectancy for men and women

    D. division of ethnic groups

    E. languages spoken

    F. literacy rates

Remember to close your paper with a complete bibliography.

   Adult check _____

                                     Initial   Date

NOUNS

el accidente de coche – the car accident
la ambulancia – the ambulance
el antibiótico – the antibiotic
la aspirina – the aspirin
el brazo – the arm
la bronquitis – the bronchitis
la cabeza – the head
el choque – the crash
la clínica – the clinic
el consultorio del médico – the doctor's office
la contusión – the bruise
el corte – the cut
la cura – the medical treatment, cure
la curita – the band-aid
el dedo – the finger
el deseo – the desire, wish
el diagnóstico – the diagnosis
el dolor – the pain
el dolor de cabeza – the headache
la enfermedad – the illness
el (la) enfermero(a) – the nurse
la escalera – the staircase, stairs
el estetoscopio – the stethoscope
la fiebre – the fever
la frente – the forehead
la garganta – the throat
la gripe – the flu, influenza
la herida – the injury, wound
el hospital – the hospital
el hueso – the bone
el jarabe para la tos – the cough syrup
la medicina – the medicine
el (la) médico(a) – the doctor
las muletas – the crutches
la muñeca – the wrist
las náuseas – the nausea
el pañuelo de papel – the tissue, kleenex
la pastilla – the pill
el pie – the foot
la pierna – the leg
la pulmonía – the pneumonia
el pulso – the pulse
los puntos – the stitches
la radiografía – the X-ray

la receta – the prescription
el reconocimiento – the (medical) examination
el resfriado – the cold (illness)
la sala de emergencias – the emergency room
la sangre – the blood
el síntoma – the symptom
la temperatura – the temperature
la tensión arterial – the blood pressure
el termómetro – the thermometer
el tobillo – the ankle
la venda – the (ace) bandage
el yeso – the cast

VERBS

aconsejar – to advise
auscultar – to listen (with a stethoscope)
caerse – to fall down
consultar a un médico – to consult a doctor
creer – to believe
darle puntos a – to give stitches to (someone)
darle vergüenza – to be ashamed
dejar de (+ infinitive) – to stop (doing something)
descansar – to rest
desear –to desire, wish
doler (o-ue) – to hurt
dudar – to doubt
enyesar – to put on a plaster cast
esperar – to hope
estar emocionado(a) – to be excited
estornudar – to sneeze
examinar – to examine
fracturar – to fracture, break
guardar cama – to stay in bed
hacerse una radiografía – to take an X-ray
mandar – to order, command
me duele(n) – it hurts (me)
mejorarse – to get better
negar (e-ie) – to deny
pedir (e-i) – to ask for
pensar (e-ie) – to think
permitir – to permit, let, allow
preferir (e-ie) – to prefer
quedarse en cama – to stay in bed
quejarse de – to complain about
querer (e-ie) – to want

recetar – to prescribe

recomendar (e-ie) – to recommend

recuperarse – to recover, recuperate

rogar (o-ue) – to beg

romperse el brazo – to break one's arm

sentarse (e-ie) – to sit down

sentir (e-ie) – to be sorry

sentirse (e-ie) – to feel

sorprenderse de – to be surprised about

sufrir – to suffer

sugerir (e-ie) – to suggest

temer – to fear

tener fiebre – to have a fever

tener miedo de – to be afraid

tener un accidente de coche – to have a car accident

tomarle el pulso – to take (someone's) pulse

tomarle la temperatura – to take (someone's)
   temperature

tomarle la tensión arterial – to take (someone's)
   blood pressure

torcerse (o-ue) – to twist, turn, sprain

toser – to cough

vendar – to bandage

vomitar – to throw up, vomit

ADJECTIVES

emocionado – excited

enfermo – sick, ill

fracturado – fractured, broken

grave – serious

hinchado – swollen

profundo – deep

roto – broken

OTHER EXPRESSIONS

es dudoso– it's doubtful

es importante – it's important

es necesario – it's necessary

es preciso – it's necessary

(no) es cierto – it's (not) certain

(no) estar seguro – it's (not) sure

Ojalá – Let's hope that, May God grant that

Pobrecito! – Poor thing!

¡Qué lástima! – What a pity!, What a shame!

¡Que se (te) mejore(s) pronto! – Hope you get better
   soon!

¡Que se (te) recupere(s) pronto! – Hope you get
   well soon!

¡Que se (te) sienta(s) mejor pronto! – Hope you feel
   better soon!